W9-AYG-788

595.7
FOW

Fowler, Allan
It's a good thing
there are insects

9680

DORN MEDIA CENTER

595.7
Fow

Rookie Read-About™ Science

It's A Good Thing There Are Insects

By Allan Fowler

Images supplied by VALAN Photos
and Jeffrey L. Rotman

Consultants:
Robert L. Hillerich, Ph.D., Bowling Green
State University, Bowling Green, Ohio

Mary Nalbandian, Director of Science,
Chicago Public Schools, Chicago, Illinois

DORN MEDIA CENTER

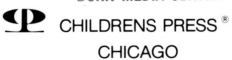

CHILDRENS PRESS®
CHICAGO

9680

'93/94

12-93 DIRECT $10.45 (CHAPTER 2)

Series cover and interior design by Sara Shelton

Library of Congress Cataloging-in-Publication Data

Fowler, Allan.
   It's a good thing there are insects / by Allan Fowler.
     p. cm.—(Rookie read-about science)
   Summary: Identifies the characteristics of insects and describes
some of their useful activities and products.
   ISBN 0-516-04905-4
   1. Insects—Juvenile literature. [1. Insects.] I. Title.
II. Series: Fowler, Allan. Rookie read-about science.
QL467.2.F68   1990
595.7—dc20
                                90-2205
                                   CIP
                                    AC

Copyright © 1990 by Childrens Press®, Inc.
All rights reserved. Published simultaneously in Canada.
Printed in the United States of America.
   3 4 5 6 7 8 9 10 R 99 98 97 96 95 94 93

Sometimes we call them bugs. But their real name is insects.

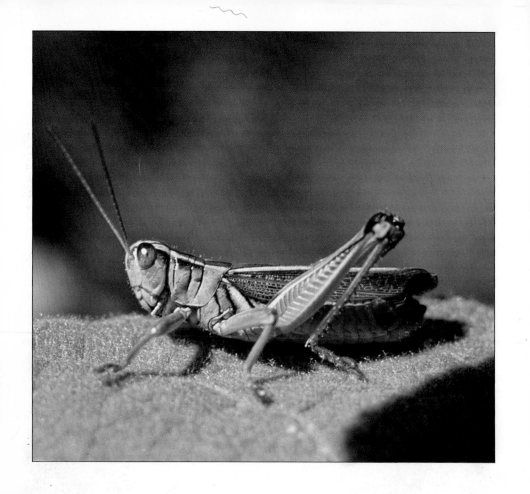

All insects have six legs
like a grasshopper.

Most insects, like flies,
have wings.

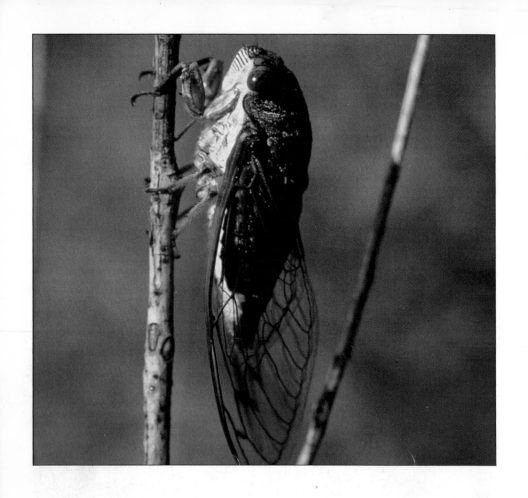

Some insects live in trees
like cicadas,

and some live in water
like water beetles.

Some insects, including most ants, make their home in the ground.

They have their own little
"town," where each ant
does its own kind of work.

A caterpillar forms a shell, called a chrysalis, around itself.

In the chrysalis, the
caterpillar changes into
a butterfly.

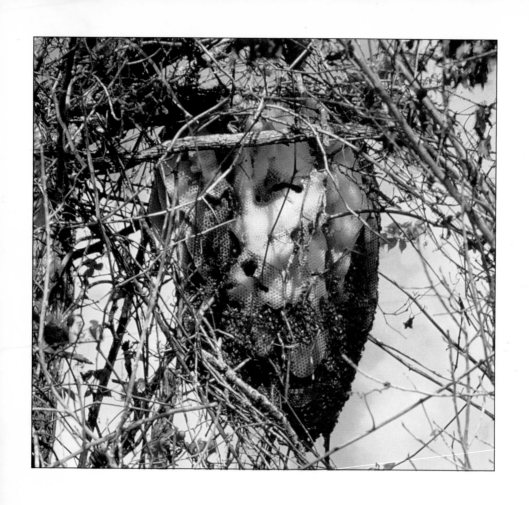

This home for bees is
called a hive.

Some insects are harmful to people.

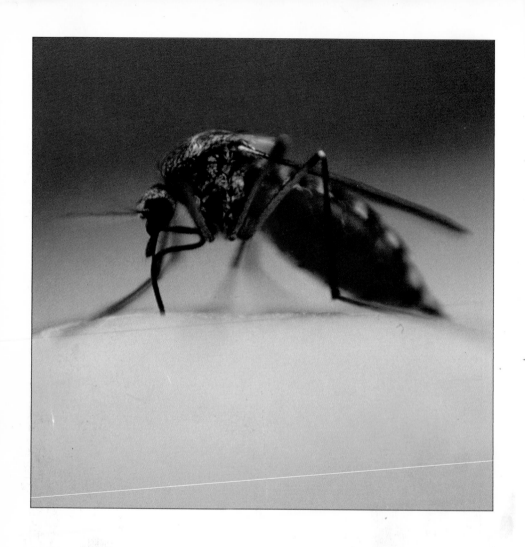

Mosquitoes can bite you.

Wasps can sting you.

Locusts can eat a farmer's crops.

But insects are helpful
to us in many ways.

We get silk from the
cocoon of a silkworm.

We get honey from
bees.

As bees fly from flower
to flower, they carry
pollen to help the flowers
grow.

Some insects are pretty
like this monarch butterfly.

Insects serve as food too.
Many animals and birds
and fish and reptiles live
by eating insects.

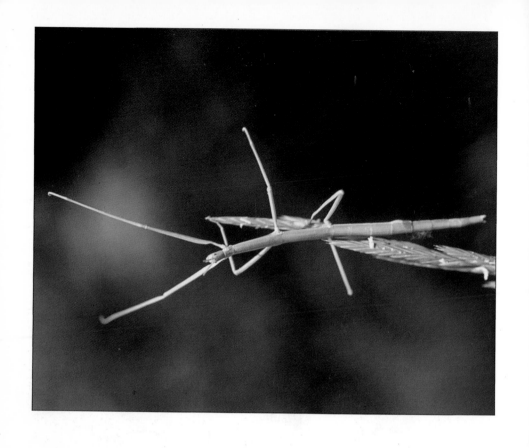

But they leave the walking
stick alone. They think
it's a twig!

Some insects glow in the dark like a firefly or a lightning bug.

DORN MEDIA CENTER

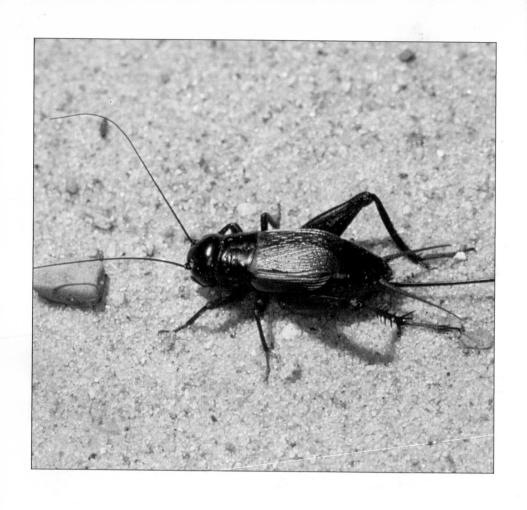

Some insects make sounds
like a cricket.

So the next time you
see a beetle

or a lady bug,

remember—it's a good
thing there are insects!

Words You Know

ants

bees
beehive

monarch
butterfly

chrysalis

cicada

cricket

fly

grasshopper

lady bug

lightning bug

locust

mosquito

silkworm cocoon

walking stick

wasp

water beetle

Index

About the Author

Allan Fowler is a free-lance writer with a background in advertising. Born in New York, he lives in Chicago now and enjoys traveling.

Photo Credits

Valan— © Herman H. Giethoorn, Cover, 4, 21, 26, 30 (top right, center right, bottom center); © Val & Alan Wilkinson, 5, 22, 24, 25, 30 (bottom left), 31 (center center & top left); © V. Whelan, 6, 28, 30 (center center & bottom right); © A. J. Bond, 7, 31 (bottom); © Kennon Cooke, 8, 30 (top left); © Dennis W. Schmidt, 9; © Pam Hickman, 10, 30 (center left); J. R. Page, 11, 14, 31 (top right); © S. J. Krasemann, 12, 16, 30 (top center), 31 (top center); © Harold V. Green, 15, 20, 31 (center right); © J. A. Wilkinson, 18, 31 (center left); © Michel Bourque, 19; © Jeff Foott, 23; © John Fowler, 27

COVER: Monarch butterfly

Dorn Elementary School
North Palos Dist. 117
Hickory Hills, IL 60457